Your Life in Print
Story by Story

Over 650 Story Starters
and Memory Joggers

Pat Cuellar

LifePrints Publishing ⚲ Auburn, California

Your Life in Print Story by Story

Pat Cuellar

Published by: LifePrints Publishing

P. O. E [Pat Cuellar / LifePrints Publishing / 432 La Costa Circle / Dayton, NV 89403] J.S.A.

Copyright © 2003 by Patricia A. Cuellar
Printed in the United States of America

Cuellar, Patricia.
    Your life in print story by story : over 650 story starters and memory joggers : you can write your life stories / by Patricia Cuellar.
    p. cm.
    ISBN 0-9729910-0-X

    1. Autobiography--Authorship--Handbooks, manuals, etc. 2. Biography as a literary form. 3. Authorship--Handbooks, manuals, etc.   I. Title

CT25.C84 2003   808'.06692
                                QB133-1577

LCCN 2003096012

Book and Cover Design: Linda McGinnis 530.623.2613

Contents

1. Why Write Your Life Stories? 7

2. Is There a Right Time to Write? 10

3. Your Writing Tools 12

4. To Tell or Not to Tell 14

5. Let's Be Sens-able 16

6. But That's Not How I Remember It! 18

7. When Writing Becomes Emotional 20

8. Your Childhood Home 22

9. Ways to Share Your Stories 24

10. Taping Your Stories 27

11. Letters are History 30

12. Your Life in Print 33

13. A Walk Down Memory Lane 40

14. Getting to Know You 42

15. Parents and Family Life 45

16. Siblings 51

17. The Growing Years 54

18. School Days 58

19. College Years 66

20. Married With (or without) Children 69

21. Grandparents 75

22. Military Life 78

23. More About You 82

24. Odd and Ends 86

25. What Do Your Remember? 91

26. The List of Lists 97

    Publications 104

    Resources 106

Foreword

When someone dies a library burns.
~ Unknown ~

We all know the most difficult part about starting something new is taking that first step. For many, just the idea of writing something that others will read is taking a huge step. I want to put your mind at ease and say that there is nothing mysterious or complicated about writing the stories of your life. This book was written especially for those who want to take that step but are not sure how or where to begin. Once you begin you will see just how easy (and enjoyable) it can be.

There are other ways to write memoirs but I've found that this approach works well for just about everyone. All you need to get started is a computer or pen and writing pad, a comfortable spot to sit and, of course, your memories. Remember that your stories are already in you. All you have to do is get them down on paper.

Take your time and enjoy the journey as you recall and write the pages of your life. Know that each story you share will be cherished for generations to come. Don't let your library burn.

Pat

Strangers in the Box

Author Unknown

Come look with me inside this drawer,
In this box I've often seen,
At the pictures, black and white,
Faces proud, still, and serene.

I wish I knew the people,
These strangers in the box,
Their names and all their memories,
Are lost among my socks.

I wonder what their lives were like,
How did they spend their days?
What about their special times?
I'll never know their ways.

If only someone had taken time,
To tell, who, what, where, and when,
These faces of my heritage,
Would come to life again.

Could this become the fate,
Of the pictures we take today?
The faces and the memories,
Someday to be passed away?

Take time to save your stories,
Seize the opportunity when it knocks,
Or someday you and yours,
Could be strangers in the box.

1

What you leave behind is not what is
engraved in stone monuments,
but what is woven into the lives of others.
~ Pericles ~

Why Write Your Life Stories?

If not you, then who? You are the only one who can write your stories! Many believe that their life hasn't been interesting enough to write about—or they wonder why anyone would want to know about their life so their stories never get written. Yet, most of us enjoy reading stories about someone's life—even those of strangers. Think what your stories will mean to those who know you, and those connected to you for generations to come. They *will* be interested and they will want to know all about you and your life.

We recently witnessed the end of the twentieth century. Think ahead one hundred years. Imagine what life will be like for your descendents at the end of this century. I imagine the world will be quite different from today. Don't you?

What do you know about the lives your ancestors led? What will your descendents know about you? Without your stories there will be nothing to know.

They will wonder about such things as:

- What did your day-to-day life involve?
- What struggles did you personally endure?
- Where did you live, work, and play?
- What schools and churches did you attend?
- What prejudices did you see or experience?
- What were your parents and grandparents like?

Writing about the past helps us to gain a better understanding of ourselves as individuals. It gives us a chance to reflect on where we've been, and how circumstances and choices have influenced us. It gives us a deeper appreciation for the struggles and victories. Writing about the past can get us back on track if we've lost sight of our goals, dreams and purpose.

This will also be true for your children's children. When written honestly, your stories will help them to better understand their world. They will identify with your fears, joys, humor, losses, failures and triumphs. They will gain an appreciation of their culture and have a sense of belonging. It's like connecting the dots on a puzzle and then discovering yourself in the center surrounded by familiar faces.

What, You're Not a Writer?

Somewhere in all of us resides a writer trying to wiggle his or her way out. It's a matter of stepping out of our comfort zone that scares us. This book offers you a safe step out of that comfort zone and gives you permission to write what you feel. There are no judgements. No one looking over your shoulder. Just you and your stories. Your book may not find its' way to a Barnes & Noble bookstore, but it *will* find its' way into your families hearts.

2

How did it get so late so soon?
It's night before it's afternoon.
December is here before it's June.
My goodness how the time has flewn.
How did it get so late so soon?

~ *Dr. Seuss* ~

Is There a Right Time to Write?

If you're the procrastinator type (like me), you probably can dream up some rational excuses for not finding time to write. Maybe you've said things like, I'll wait until I retire or after the garage is cleaned out and the closets are organized. Or, I'll wait until the kids are grown and out of the house.

That last excuse is mine, and I can tell you that it doesn't work. For years it seemed as though one or the other of our six kids was either flying in or flying out of the house, and the garage is still a mess.

Try to find time that's best for you. Maybe you're a morning person and can fit in twenty or thirty minutes before your day begins. Maybe just before going to sleep when everything is quiet. Carry your notebook with you and write a few sentences during lunch hour.

Finding time is a challenge, but we all make time for things that are important to us. And, although there may not be a right time to write, *now* is a great time to begin.

3

*I think I did pretty well, considering I started
out with a bunch of blank paper.*

~ Steve Martin ~

Your Writing Tools

This list will help you get started and stay organized
as you watch your collection of stories grow.

- ☐ Computer, typewriter or pen and paper
- ☐ Laser or inkjet printer
- ☐ Large three-hole loose-leaf binder
- ☐ Red pens for making changes
- ☐ Colored file folders
- ☐ Colored tabbed page dividers
- ☐ Acid-free paper and sheet protectors
- ☐ An unabridged dictionary
- ☐ Several small notebooks

The loose-leaf binder is for holding stories that you are working on and have completed. The tabbed dividers are to separate your finished pages from the unfinished pages. Colored or specially marked folders are to divide and categorize relevant periods in your life. For instance:

Childhood (1-12)
Adolescence (13-18)
Early Adulthood (19-25)
Adulthood (26-64)
Later years (65-present)

Notebooks are to keep next to your bed, in your car, your purse or backpack. You never know when an "Oh, yeah, I remember" moment might occur. Don't trust those moments to memory. Jot them down.

If you should find yourself without a notebook you can always write on a paper napkin or a scrap of paper. Just make sure you file it in your folder before it gets tossed in the washer (a hint that comes from personal experience).

A small tape recorder can help eliminate the need to keep paper and pen handy. Remember to keep fresh batteries on hand.

We all have the right to tell the truth
about our own life.
~ Unknown ~

To Tell or Not to Tell

In order for your family to benefit from your stories it is important to be truthful. If you find yourself at a crossroad, not knowing whether to tell or not to tell something, ask yourself these questions. Is this information important for me to share? Is this some thing they need to know? Why do I want others to know?

I'll share what has worked for me and perhaps it will help you if a similar situation should arise. Whatever you're questioning, write it down in great detail. Set it aside for at least two weeks before you read what you've written. The time lapse between writing and reading will help you to be more objective.

Once you've read what you've written, ask yourself the same questions one more time:

Is this information important to share?
Is it something they need to know?
Why do I want to others to know?

The why question is very important to answer especially if what you write might affect others in a negative way.

5

Before you can inspire with emotion,
you must be swamped with it yourself.
Before you can move their tears,
your own must flow. To convince them,
you must yourself believe.
~ Winston Churchill ~

Let's Be Sens-able

You want your book to be more than just facts; you want it to come to life. When you write your stories using all your senses—sight, smell, touch, sound and taste you breathe life into them. Senses create moods and images that will draw your readers in.

The Sense of Taste and Smell

Taste and smell can trigger both physical and emotional responses. For instance, have you ever tasted something that activated a physical reaction? How about an odor that triggered a forgotten memory? William McFee, an author noted for his nautical writings wrote, "There is nothing like an odor to stir memories."

Sight, Sound, and Touch

These senses are much easier to describe since they're more tangible. The following sentence is one example of combining sight, sound, and touch.

I stood on the rocks, soaked, wet and scared. I couldn't see through the dense fog, and the only sound I heard was the blare of a foghorn.

Using Anecdotes

What are some of the hilarious and embarrassing moments in your life? We all have them and somehow never forget them—or others won't let us forget them. Sprinkling your stories with anecdotes adds flavor to your stories. They also can reveal a lot about you and your personality.

The following is an anecdote from the late humorist and charismatic entertainer, Victor Borge, about the youngest of his five children. His little boy had been invited to a birthday party where everyone was to go swimming. When the little boy returned, his father asked him,

"Did you have a good time?"
"Yes, father."
"Did you have ice cream and cake?"
"Yes, father."
"Did you go swimming?"
"Yes, Father."
"Were there more boys than girls swimming?"
"I don't know. They didn't have their clothes on."

Why not share the hilarious or embarrassing moments in your life?

*When I was younger, I could remember
anything, whether it had happened or not.*
~ Mark Twain ~

But That's Not How I Remember It!

Have you shared an experience with someone who recalled it differently than you did? No matter how memorable an experience shared by two or more people may be, it's not unusual to have very different interpretations. Memories are malleable and shift over time, people remember things in different ways. That doesn't mean that anyone's recollection is wrong—just different.

A simple example is a childhood memory that differs from my good friend Meg. As youngsters Meg and I would clamp metal roller skates to our shoes, tighten them with a special key, and then tear down steep neighborhood driveways at break-neck speed. At least that's what I recall.

Years later as Meg and I were reminiscing, I brought up the driveways that we risked our lives on. When she finally stopped laughing, she informed me that those so-called breathtaking driveways were just mere slopes in the concrete. But how could that be?

When you write a recollection and someone recalls it differently, that's okay. The important thing is for you to write it the way you remember it.

7

I don't really understand my own life
until I have storied it
and told it to someone else.

~ Unknown ~

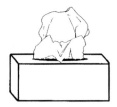

When Writing Becomes Emotional

Bad things do happen to good people. No one is immune to pain and struggle. As you write you may revisit some painful times. It may be divorce, loss of a loved one, chronic illness, or an emotional struggle. How will you handle these emotional moments when they arise? Will you write about them or choose to leave them out?

Donna, a workshop participant, shared the anxiety and anger she had following an unexpected divorce that left her with two small children. She said, "Although I still get angry at times, writing about it gives me a safe way to vent and accept it."

When I lost my daughter, who was a young mother, writing gave me solace and joy. I wrote stories about her, not only for myself but also for my granddaughter. I wanted her to know every little thing about her mother— her growing-up years, her joys, her dreams, and the special connection and friendship we shared. These stories gave my granddaughter a stronger sense of being part of her mother's life and a chance to know her—not only as her mother but also as someone very much like herself.

Don't be afraid to write about the tough times. When we express thoughts, worry, hurt, or unresolved issues onto paper the burden is lightened a little, clearing a space that can help us to move on.

Memory allows us to recall the people we've known, the places we've been, the music we listened to, and the things we've done.

~ Unknown ~

Your Childhood Home

This section is fun and it will stir up some long forgotten memories. So grab some paper and a pencil and put on some old tunes. You're about to revisit your childhood home.

Etch a Sketch

Don't be concerned if you're not artistic. No artistic ability is necessary here—just your memories.

Begin by sketching an overhead view of your childhood home as if you were looking down into it without a roof. Next, mark the location of doors, windows, and walls. Show where you shared family meals, where your bed was placed in your room, and where you did your homework. How about that hiding place or your favorite room?

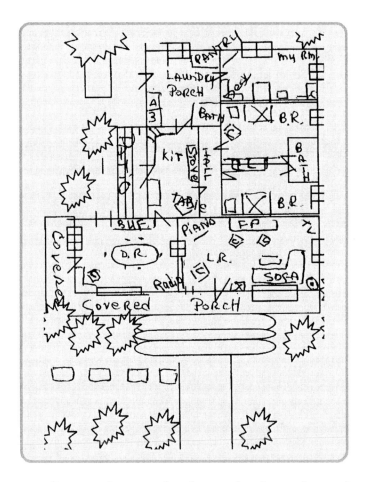

Once you've completed your sketch, you're ready to invite the grandchildren over for an imaginary tour. As they enter the front door begin to talk about (jot down) the things you see and remember as if they were walking beside you. You may want to revisit the backyard, walk through the neighborhood, or go to the corner store.

You'll be surprised at the memories you recall, and how much fun it will be for you and for your grandchildren to visit your childhood home.

My life has been a tapestry of rich
and royal hue, an everlasting
vision of the everchanging view.
~ Carole King ~

Ways to Share Your Stories

Once you've written, or while in the process of writing, you may want to share your stories with loved ones. There are many interesting ways to accomplish this. Here are a few ideas.

Anniversary Album

This takes time but it's worth it and fun to create. Gather photographs of homes and cars you've owned, the church where you were married, or favorite vacations. Once you've chosen your photographs write a short story or an anecdote around each one and create a personal cover. Use this idea for a parent's anniversary or Grandparent's Day. Even one photograph can tell a great story.

Birthdays and Graduations

A special day deserves a special gift. It can be as simple and heartwarming as recalling a favorite story or memory of him or her. If you're poetic, write a verse or two about the receiver on decorative paper or a card.

Religious Holidays

This is a great time to exchange stories with family members. You may have to encourage others a bit, but if you create a theme such as, "What is your most memorable childhood holiday?" it will be easy. A story exchange can be more meaningful than expensive gifts.

Family Reunions

We all like taking photographs at reunions but how about adding something a little different? At your next reunion have everyone write a paragraph or two about their life, their family or their thoughts of the day. Very young children can contribute by drawing pictures. Supply the paper and pens. Following the reunion collect the stories and pictures. Recruit two or three family members to help put an album together before the next reunion. Make copies for everyone and don't forget to include your own story.

Specialty Cards

For a milestone birthday I received a great photo card from an old schoolmate. On the front my friend had reproduced a photo of us in our prom dresses. On the inside was a humorous and satiric reminiscence. This was something I definitely saved for my life stories. What ideas can you come up with?

Career

Have you had an interesting, unusual, or high-profile career? Were you a store owner, rancher, truck driver, pilot, or teacher? Maybe you've had more than one career or made a mid-life career change. Were you a stay-at-home mom who has adventures to share about raising children? Include details, anecdotes, the up and downs and what you career choice meant to you.

Two more ideas

If you're a gourmet cook (or not), how about including a story that revolves around food? Remember to share your favorite recipe. Are you a crafter? Share a favorite craft idea and include the instructions. Don't forget to mention any contests or awards you've received and what it meant to you.

One More . . .

Do you have a hand-me-down or something extra special that you treasure? Write a story around it. For instance, I once wrote a short story about an old pewter music box that belonged to my grandparents. As a child I would love to go into their bedroom, wind the key and listen to it play, "Button Up Your Overcoat". I have that music box today and every once in awhile I wind the key and remember.

Just One More . . .

Consider donating your book to your local library or making it available to the Genealogical Societies Ancestral Files. Remember, you are part of history.

10

Story is far older than the art of science and psychology, and will always be the elder in the equation no matter how much time passes.
-Clarissa Pinkola Estes-

Taping Your Stories

You may choose to audio tape your life stories and transcribe them later for printing into a book. Preserving your stories on audio or videotape is an intimate way to communicate with your family. Here are some things you'll want to do before you begin taping.

❑ Make a list of story topics you want to cover.

❑ Make a sublist highlighting the key points within that topic so you won't forget any important details.

❑ Find a comfortable spot to sit where the recorder and microphone are close to you and on a stable surface.

❑ Make sure the area where you are taping is free from intrusive sounds such as the humming of a refrigerator or traffic noise. Even the innocent chirping of a bird can be distracting on tape.

❑ Use an external microphone that can be placed on a table or one that attaches to your clothing. This leaves your hands free and you're able to sit or stand without having to talk directly into a recorder.

❑ Use a high-quality, sixty-minute audiotape.

❑ Label each tape with the day, year, and subject.

❑ State your name at the beginning of each tape.

Transcribing Hints

❑ Type only one or two sentences or a short segment at a time.

❑ Begin new paragraphs at natural breaking points.

❑ Convert sentence fragments into whole sentences.

❑ Leave out the "uhs" and the "you knows" as you transcribe.

❑ One hour of taping will take two to four hours to transcribe.

❑ Make hard copies of your transcription as well as saving to storage media.

❑ To avoid losing a file, save more than one copy.

Speech Recognition Software

This is a great invention, especially for those who find it difficult to sit or type at a keyboard for any length of time. All you do with speech recognition software is speak into a microphone. You do, however, need to give punctuation and formatting commands as you go along. The software converts your speech directly into computer text. It is relatively inexpensive and available at office supply stores.

Keep in Mind

Videotapes begin to deteriorate in ten to twelve years. CDs, once described as being indestructible are vulnerable to stray magnetic fields, humidity, oxidation and decay. Technology, as we know it today, will probably be obsolete in a very few years. Think how quickly audio cassettes are vanishing. Remember 8-track movies? Many major computer companies no longer include a floppy disc drive on standard computer equipment. Technology changes, but the written word will always be around. To be on the safe side, put your words in print.

11

Letters are History

Over the years I have saved letters received from family and friends, and also made copies of letters written to them. These letters have served as a wonderful resource and reference for my memoirs. Letters add historical content and valuable family information.

Before you mail off a letter you've written make a copy. Years later you'll enjoy reading it and you'll be amazed at how much has transpired in your life.

Since the advent of fax and e-mail the personal handwritten message is becoming increasingly rare. Although it's nice to receive mail in any form, there is something very special about finding a letter from an old friend in the mailbox.

But all this technology has its upside. It gives us a way to reconnect with long-lost friends and make new ones in every corner of the world. The next time you receive a personal e-mail hit the print button and save them in a binder. It's another way of journaling.

Envelopes

Keep the envelopes from old letters. They hold a wealth of information such as address, year, and place of origin. The data will come in handy if you ever conduct a genealogical search.

Invitations

Do you have old invitations, personal notes, or paper clippings stuffed in boxes somewhere? How about old baby announcements and special gift cards? Some are very ornate and unusual. Consider making copies and scanning a few into your book.

Foreign Text

What do you do with letters written in a language other than English? I've kept letters written by and to my grandfather from relatives in Europe. The problem was, I didn't have a clue to what they said.

Eager to understand what was written I searched for Web sites that could translate my treasure. The site I use most often is www.freetranslation.com. There are other sites, and most translate words, books, or entire sites. Amazing!

Creating a Book of Letters

So what do you do with all those letters you saved from family and friends? Why not compile them into a book? Here's a simple and inexpensive way to create a book of letters.

- Arrange letters and envelopes by their dates. Oldest first.

- Open letters so they can easily be read.

- Slip the items into an acid-free sheet protector.

- Place any translations next to the original.

- Place the envelope alongside the letter.

- If dates and addresses are not clear, print them on a separate card and place the card next to the subject.

- For added interest place a photo or a related item alongside the letter.

- Write a title for your book.

- Add your name (as the creator) and where and when it was published.

- Write a preface telling a little about your book and how it came about.

- If you like, include an acknowledgment page to thank those who contributed to the book.

12

*All good writing is swimming underwater
and holding your breath.*

-F. Scott Fitzgerald-

Your Life in Print

Once you've poured your heart and soul into writing your stories it's time to get them into print. You don't want to shove them into a drawer for paper mites to feast on—you want to share them with loved ones. On the following pages we'll discuss ways you can accomplish this.

How Big Should My Book Be?

This is one question I'm often asked. The number of pages or the method of printing your book is not important. It can be a 20-page booklet produced on your computer or a 300-page hardcover book produced by a publisher. It all depends on how much you want to say and why you are writing. While many of us write to leave stories for our children and grandchildren, others write just for themselves. They want to get their thoughts, feelings, observations, etc. on paper as much as those who write for others. The size of your book is not important. The fact that you are taking time to write is what matters.

Whether you write ten pages or one hundred, here are some things to include:

❑ Title of your book and subtitle (if any)

❑ Your name as the author

❑ Copyright symbol and year (see copyright page)

❑ Table of contents (arrange pages, chapters or stories, as you want them to appear in your book).

❑ List of photographs and maps (for quick reference place them after the table of contents).

❑ An introduction to your book

❑ Dedications (can be placed in the introduction)

❑ Ancestral chart if available

❑ An ending composed of an affectionate line or message if desired

What About Editing?

If spelling, grammar and punctuation are a concern then it's a good idea to have someone edit your work. When we get immersed in our own work errors can easily be overlooked. If the cost of having your work edited is prohibitive, try to recruit an English student or a family member to help.

Although these elements are important, you don't want your concern to get in the way of your writing—or have it stop you from writing. Your descendants will not be looking for errors. They are only interested in what you have to say.

Many years ago my great uncle, at the age of 87, wrote a dozen pages of family history in his own words. It was not perfectly written, in fact, he wrote with his left hand since his right was crippled with arthritis. He was not concerned with perfection, only in sharing what he knew with his family. He wrote, "I'm writing this because I want the young people to know a little about their heritage." Just those few pages meant a lot to us.

There is one more point I'd like to mention in regards to editing. Actually, it's a point that took me a very long time to learn. *Do not edit as you write.* When you edit as you write, it breaks the flow of your thoughts and it will take twice as long to write your story. Wait until your story is completed, then add or delete as you see fit. Then:

- Read them out loud. Hearing words spoken helps you to pick up on areas that need clarity.
- Double-check the spelling of names and places.
- Double check days, months and years.
- Don't fret over the little stuff.

Working With a Printer

Here are some things to do and ask before hiring a printer.

❑ Determine the number of copies you need.

❑ What do you want the book to look like?

❑ Can the printer provide the cover and the binding?

❑ Ask to see examples of the printer's work.

❑ In what format does the printer need your work?

❑ Get several quotes.

❑ Get everything in writing.

Print-on-Demand Publishers (POD)

Print-on-demand publishing companies are able to print one book or one thousand—as many as you need. Once they are stored digitally, they can produce your order quickly. There is a onetime setup fee, and the cost can be higher per book than other printing options. Contact POD publishers for more information (see resource page).

Doing it All Yourself

If you only need a few copies of your book, and you don't want to engage a printer or a POD publisher, you can create the book yourself. Once your book is completed, have the pages photocopied and bound at a copy center such as Kinko's. Larger copy centers have a variety of bindings to choose from and can help you determine the correct binding for the number of pages you have. You can also run copies on your home printer. Here are some hints for writing and coping your book on your computer and printer.

❏ Use a laser printer for best quality.

❏ Use good quality acid-free paper.

❏ Leave extra space on the inside margin for binding.

❏ Indent your paragraphs or separate them with a blank line.

❏ Use 1½ line spacing for easier reading.

❏ Number the pages.

❏ Always keep a hardcopy as an original

Should You Copyright Your Book?

Your memoirs are automatically protected once they have been created and fixed in a tangible form. You do not need a formal copyright, however, obtaining a copyright is a simple and inexpensive procedure and I encourage you to get one.

The copyright application form (Short Form TX) is available from the U. S. Copyright Office. You can mail in a request, or call their 24-hour forms hotline. Your library may have forms or you can download one from the Copyright Office www.copyright.gov/faq.html.

To register your work, the following three items are required by the Copyright Office.

1. A properly completed application (Form TX).

2. A nonrefundable filing fee of $30 for each application. (Check for fee changes).

3. A nonreturnable copy of the work being registered. (Do not send your only copy).

Send these three items in the same envelope or package to:

Library of Congress, Copyright Office
101 Independence Avenue, S.E.
Washington, D. C. 20559-6000

If you think your memoirs may have commercial possibilities then you will need to purchase an ISBN (International Standard Book Number). An ISBN is a worldwide identification system. It uniquely identifies books and identifies one title or edition from another. If you want to learn more about publishing I recommend, *The Self-Publishing Manual—How to Write, Print and Sell Your Own Book,* by Dan Poynter.

Using Photographs

Most of us have taken, inherited and accumulated hundreds of family photos in our lifetime, and they all have a special meaning. It would be impossible to include them all. Your task will be to narrow your selection down to a handful that are relevant to your stories. That's not always easy to do since you'll have many favorites.

Once your selection is made, there are different ways to display them. You can place the photo on the page where you want it to be and have it scanned. You can do this throughout the book or you can group your photographs on a few pages and have them set into the center of the book.

Colored photographs can be copied in black and white. Colored scanning is expensive but if you want to use colored photos, you can group them as mentioned above to save scanning cost. You'll only be charged for the page, not each photo.

As you include each photograph identify them with as much detail as possible.

- Who is in the photograph?

- What is taking place?

- Where and when was the photo taken?

- What do you remember about the people?

- What buildings do you recognize?

13

*There is awareness inside us
that won't come out until we start writing.*

~ Unknown ~

A Walk Down Memory Lane

On the following pages you'll find hundreds of story starters and memory joggers to help you write your life stories. Although most questions can be answered with one or two words, you'll want to give as much detail as possible to make your stories interesting and informative.

You can easily combine questions and create a paragraph or a story. For instance:

On July 4, 1940 I was born to Marie Rose McAllister and John Michael Adams at Memorial Hospital in Pittsburgh, Pennsylvania. My mother had just graduated from high school and my dad was working at a local grocery store when they married in 1938. I now live in Jasper, Wyoming with my husband, David Lee Anderson. We met in high school when we were . . .

Don't feel compelled to answer each and every question. Many may not pertain to your life. A good way to begin is to first go through the list and circle the ones you want to respond to. Although many topics are covered, you will no doubt have some of your own to add. One memory will trigger another.

You may find some questions quite personal and some frivolous. Give only as much information as you feel comfortable giving. If you write about the good, the bad, the ugly, and the humorous, your stories will be honest and real.

You can start at the beginning of the list or skip around. You can answer all the questions or select just one and write a delightful story around it. Even *one* story will make a lasting and treasured gift.

Here are a few places to look to get you started on that walk down memory lane:

- School year books
- Jewelry boxes
- Junk drawers
- Titles on your bookshelf
- Old record albums and sheet music
- Certificates, awards and documents
- Old letters, cards and ticket stubs
- Postcards and photo albums
- A visit to you old neighborhood
- Old newspapers and magazines

14

*Every man is a quotation
from all his ancestors.*
~ Ralph Waldo Emerson ~

Getting to Know You

1. What is your full birth name?

2. What is the month, day, and year of your birth?

3. What day of the week and time of day were you born?

4. What race and religion are you?

5. What was your weight and length at birth?

6. What color was your hair at birth? Was it curly or straight?

7. What immunizations have you had?

8. What childhood illnesses have you had?

9. What is your blood type?

10. Are you nearsighted or farsighted? What color are you eyes?

11. Do you have any hearing problems?

12. Do you have any physical disabilities?

13. Do you have any birthmarks?

14. In what city, county and state (country) were you born?

15. Were you born in a hospital or at home?

16. If a hospital, what was the name of the hospital and its' location?

17. Was it a private, public, or military hospital?

18. What was the doctor's name who delivered you?

19. If a midwife attended your birth, what was her name? What do you know about her?

20. Were you born somewhere other than in a hospital or at home? Where?

21. Were there any complications during your birth? What were they?

22. Were you named after a family member or someone special? Who?

23. Who was in the delivery room with your mother?

24. Where did you go first upon leaving the hospital?

25. Who brought you and your mother home from the hospital?

26. What is your astrological sign? Flower? Birthstone?

27. Did a regional, national, or international event occur on the day of your birth?

28. Who was president when you were born?

29. Are you a twin? Are you a fraternal or maternal twin? Were you the first or second to be born? How many minutes apart were you born?

30. Were you adopted? At what age were you adopted?

31. How old were your adoptive parents when they brought you home?

32. What were the circumstances of your adoption?

33. What do you know about your birth parents? Do you stay in contact with them?

34. How old were you when you were told of your adoption?

35. How did being adopted affect you or your life?

36. How did you feel and what did you think when you were told?

37. Were there other siblings at home at the time of your adoption?

38. Would you consider being an adoptive parent?

15

Family faces are magic mirrors.
Looking at people who belong to us,
we see the past, present and future.
~ Gail Lumet Buckley ~

Your Parents and Family Life

1. What is your mother's full name?

2. What was her maiden name?

3. What is your father's full name?

4. What is your mother's and father's date of birth?

5. In what city, county, and state were they born?

6. Was one or both of your parents born in another country? Which country? Why and when did they come to America? How or from what port did they enter the U.S.? Do they talk about it?

7. How many grandchildren and great grandchildren do your parents have?

8. How and when did your parents meet? How long did they know each other before they married?

9. What is their anniversary date? How long have they been married?

10. Was this the first marriage for both? If not, what do you know about their first marriage?

11. Are both parents still living? If not, when did he or she pass away? How old were they? How old were you at the time?

12. Did your parents have nicknames? By what name did you call them?

13. What sort of work did your father do? Where did he work? How many years did he work? How old was he when he retired? Was he ever out of work?

14. Did your mother work outside the home? What was her job?

15. If your mother worked outside the home was there someone at home when you returned from school?

16. Did you attend an after school supervised program? Did you care for yourself?

17. Did you have a special relationship with one parent? What made it special?

18. How would you describe your parents' personalities? Did they have a sense of humor or were they the quiet type?

19. What is the most vivid memory you have of your father and mother?

20. What do you remember about their home and yard? What style furniture did they have? Was it a formal or casual setting?

21. What modern appliances did they purchase? What was their favorite? Do you know what they paid for the appliances?

22. When did they buy their first television? What was the make, screen size and cost?

23. Did deliverymen bring ice, coal, heating fuel, milk or other products to the house?

24. What inventions did they see develop in their lifetime?

25. What make and model car did your parents own? Did your mother drive?

26. Did you ever see your parents cry? Do you know the reason?

27. What made your parents the most angry? What made them the most proud?

28. What lessons and values did your parents teach you? How did those values and lessons shape your life?

29. What family myths have come down to you from your parents and grandparents?

30. What features or habits did you inherit from your parents?

31. In what ways are you like your mother or father?

32. Would you consider your parents strict or easygoing?

33. How did your parents discipline you and your siblings?

34. What chores did you have around the house? Which ones did you most dislike?

35. Did your family take yearly vacations? Where was their favorite place to go?

36. Did you take family camping, fishing, or hunting trips?

37. What is your special vacation memory?

38. Did you and your family ever go abroad? Where to? How old were you?

39. What is your family's religious belief? Do you practice that same belief today?

40. What was the name and location of the church, temple, or place of worship your family attended? Did you regularly attend Sunday school or take religious training?

41. Were you christened as a child? How old were you?

42. Who did they select as your Godparents? What are their names? Where do they live? Have you stayed close to them?

43. What other religious rites have you received?

44. Did you have a favorite pastor or rabbi? What was his or her name? Did they ever visit your home or come to dinner?

45. Is anyone in your family a member of the clergy?

46. What are the names of your aunts, uncles, and cousins? Where do they live? Who has the largest family?

47. Did your family hold yearly reunions? Where did they usually take place? Did everyone try to attend? Do you still have reunions today?

48. What family story is sure to be told at every family reunion?

49. Which relative do you consider to be the life of the party? Why?

50. Which relatives did you like spending time with? Which one is special to you?

51. Do you have a famous relative? Do you have a relative that is especially talented? What do they do?

52. Did you have pets while you were growing up? What kind and what were their names? Who cared for them? Where did they sleep? Did you ever have a pet die?

53. In your parents' home who managed the money? Did you receive an allowance?

54. Did your parents save for your college education or were you expected to pay your own way?

55. Was grace said before each meal? Who led the family in grace?

56. Were meals eaten at the kitchen or dining room table? Who was responsible for setting the table and cleaning up after meals?

57. Was there a lot of conversation at mealtime or was it quiet? Did discussions usually revolve around a particular topic?

58. Were you allowed to watch television or listen to music during meals?

59. Did your family frequent restaurants or only on special occasions? Did you or your parents have a favorite restaurant?

60. Was there a lot of laughter or music in your home? Who had the best sense of humor—your mother or father?

61. Did the family listen to radio or watch television together? Did you play cards or other table games together? What game was your favorite?

16

*What I want is to plunge my hand
into a lucky dip and come up
with a handful of assorted memories.*

~ *Agatha Christie* ~

Siblings

1. How many sisters and brothers do you have? What are their names and dates of birth?

2. What birth order do you hold in the family? Did you enjoy or ever take advantage of your position in the family?

3. What expectations did your parents have of you and your siblings?

4. Did you get along with your siblings? Do you get along with them now?

5. What things did you like to do with your brothers and sisters? Did you tend to get into trouble together?

6. Which sibling were you especially close to? What made the relationship special?

7. Was there a sibling who was protective of you? Do you remember any particular time when protection was needed? Were you protective of them?

8. What nickname or special name did they like to call you? Did you like or dislike the name?

9. Did one or more sibling tease you a lot? Who teased you the most? What did they tease you about and how did you react to it?

10. Did you attend the same schools? Did teachers ever compare you with another sibling?

11. Did you help each other with homework or chores? Did you ever cover for them when something went wrong? Do you remember what it was about?

12. Did you ever borrow each other's clothes and jewelry? Did you or they borrow things without asking?

13. What size dress, pants, and shoes did you wear at age sixteen?

14. Did you share a room with a sibling? Did you want to have your own room? If you shared, who decided how it was decorated? What did you have on the walls?

15. If you have a twin sister or brother, what do you like most about being a twin? What do you like least?

16. Did being a twin affect your life in any way? How?

17. Did your mother dress you alike? Did people make frequent comments about you and your twin? Did their comments make you feel special or was it annoying?

18. Did your parents divorce? Did they remarry making you a stepchild?

19. What were the circumstance and how did you feel about the situation?

20. Do you have stepsisters or brothers? What are their names and birth dates?

21. Did you get along with them? Did it take you a long time to adjust and accept each other? What is your relationship with them today?

22. What was most difficult about having a stepsister or stepbrother and being a stepchild?

23. Did you live together full time or on designated days? How did that work out for everyone? Did you have to travel to spend time with a parent?

24. Were holidays celebrated together?

17

*He is the happiest man who can draw
an unbroken connection between
the end of life and the beginning.*

~ Goethe ~

The Growing Years

1. Did you have a tricycle? Did you have a bicycle? What brand was it? What did it look like? What accessories did it have?

2. Did you ride your bike to school? Where did you most like to ride and with whom? Did a parent always know where you were?

3. Did you have a savings account or a special place to save your money? What things did you save for? What things did you like to buy with your money?

4. Did you like to read as a child? What sorts of books were your favorites?

5. Did you like to read comic books? Who was your favorite comic book character?

6. Did you like to play dress-up? What was your favorite Halloween costume?

7. Did you have a special doll that you played with? What did you name her? Do you still have her?

8. Did you like to play cops and robbers or cowboys and Indians as a child? Did you use toy guns? Did you like to play the good guy or bad guy?

9. What was your favorite toy? Did you collect baseball or other types of cards? Did you keep any?

10. Did you build model cars or airplanes, fly kites, ride scooters and roller skate?

11. What was your favorite hobby?

12. Did you have a playhouse or a tree house? Who built it for you?

13. What sidewalk or street games did you play? Did you play hide-and-seek, tag, jump rope, jacks, or marbles?

14. Were there a lot of children in your neighborhood to play with? Who was your best friend in the neighborhood?

15. Did you like to stay out after dark to play with friends? Were you ever afraid of the dark? What was it that frightened you? Did you live on a safe, dangerous, or busy street?

16. What was the worst injury you ever received as a child? What happened?

17. Did your parents like your friends? Were you ever forbidden to see any of them? What was the reason?

18. Where did you and your friends like to congregate in the neighborhood?

19. Which childhood friends do you keep in touch with?

20. Did you collect photographs of athletes or movie stars? Did you belong to any fan clubs? Which ones?

21. Did you have a hero as a child? What did you like about him or her?

22. What adult did you look up to as a child? Why?

23. What kind of music did you like to listen to? What was your favorite radio or TV show?

24. What holidays did you like the best? What made them special?

25. Did you have Easter egg hunts?

26. Did you have birthday parties? What party do you remember the most? Do you remember who attended?

27. Did you have sleepovers with friends? What did you like to do?

28. How did you like to spend your weekends?

29. What was your favorite food and beverage? What was your favorite TV dinner? Do you remember the brand?

30. Did you like to eat a lot of sweets? What was your favorite ice cream flavor and favorite pastry?

31. Did you like to camp out in your backyard?

32. Did you take dancing lessons? What type of dancing?

33. What musical instrument did you play? Did you practice willingly or did you need to be coaxed?

34. What sports did you participate in when you were in grammar school?

35. What silly sayings do you remember from your childhood?

36. Were you ever rebellious? In what ways?

37. Did you ever run away (or think about running away) from home? Why? Where did you go and for how long were you gone? What occurred afterward?

38. What was your favorite color?

39. Did you ever dream of becoming famous? What did you dream of becoming?

18

*Friends are the siblings
that God never gave us.*

~ Unknown ~

School Days

1. What do you remember about your first day at school? How old were you when you first began?

2. Did you want to go to school or be at home? Were you excited or frightened about going?

3. Did you attend preschool and kindergarten? Do you remember the names of the schools and their locations?

4. What time did you begin your preschool or kindergarten day? Who took you and picked you up?

5. How far did you live from your grammar and high school? How did you get there each day?

6. Did you take a lunch or use the cafeteria? Who packed your lunch? Did you ever trade lunches with friends?

7. Did you attend a private, religious, or public school? Were you home-schooled?

8. Did your class pledge allegiance to the Flag or pray before class? Were morning physical exercises held?

9. Do you remember the names of your grammar school and high school principal or the names of any of your teachers?

10. What are the names and locations of the elementary and high school you attended? Are they still being used today? Have you ever revisited them since graduating?

11. Did you have a high school mascot? What are the school's colors? Do you remember your high school song or cheers?

12. Did you purchase a class ring and yearbook? Do you still have them? Have you gone through your yearbook since graduating? What do you think when you see the photos and read remarks written by your classmates?

13. What did you like or dislike most about your high school social life?

14. What classes did you like and dislike the most? Why?

15. Was schoolwork difficult or relatively easy for you? Did anyone help you with your homework? How much time did you spend on homework each day?

16. Did you spend much time at the library? Were you always prepared for exams or did you procrastinate and then cram the night before?

17. What was the most difficult subject for you to grasp? Did you ever have a tutor?

18. Did you consider yourself to be an excellent, good, average or poor student? Did you parents expect you to earn good grades?

19. Were you rewarded or punished for your grades? Did you ever sign your parent's name to a report card?

20. Were you often late for classes? Did you ever cut school? What did you do when you cut? Were you ever caught? What happened?

21. Do you still remember the first thing you had to memorize? Was memorizing difficult or easy for you?

22. Did you read or recite in front of the class or the student body? Did it make you nervous or anxious?

23. Did your school or class hold spelling bees or other academic contests? Were you good at them?

24. Did you ever study a foreign language? Were you able to use it after graduation or do you just remember certain phrases?

25. Did you have a memorable teacher or mentor? What made him or her memorable?

26. What teacher was the most intimidating and why? How did you handle it?

27. Did you keep any of your grammar or high school papers or artwork? Do you know where they are today? Have you ever shown them to your children?

28. How did teachers discipline the students? Were you ever sent to the principal's office? Were you ever suspended from school? For what reason and what resulted?

29. Was there a school bully? Did the bully ever pick on you? Did you fight back? Did you stand up for those who were bullied? Did anyone stand up for you?

30. Were you ever called or did you ever call anyone bad names? What names were used?

31. What was your most embarrassing moment in school? What were the circumstances? Were you often teased about it?

32. Did you belong to a clique? If not, did you feel left out?

33. What organizations or clubs did you belong to in high school? Were you a class officer, cheerleader, or majorette?

34. Did you belong to a drama or music club? Were you a performer or part of the stage crew? What did you like about being part of a group?

35. Were you a member of the school band? Did you belong to or have a band of your own? What type of music did you play. Where did you practice?

36. Did you attend homecoming events? Were you a homecoming queen or king or part of the court? What activities took place during homecoming week?

37. Were you ever described as the teacher's pet or the class clown? How did you like the label? How were you treated?

38. Did you work on the school newspaper or in the school office? What did you do?

39. Did you have school lockers with combination locks? What did you keep in your locker? Was it neat or messy most of the time?

40. Did you attend school athletic events? Which sport was your favorite?

41. In what sport did you participate? Did you belong to a team? How important was it to be part of a team?

42. Did you participate in off-campus sports, such as local softball or soccer leagues? Did a parent coach a team you played on?

43. Did you work hard to excel at sports or did you just enjoy the game and being part of the team? Did you receive any trophies or ribbons?

44. Do you remember going on classroom field trips? What was your favorite? Did your school hold carnivals or bake sales?

45. Did you ever have beach parties with your friends? What beach did you go to? Did you like to surf, water ski, or swim?

46. Did you take snow skiing trips? Where did you go to ski? How old were you when you learned how to ski?

47. Who was your best friend in grammar school and in high school? Is he or she still your friend today?

48. How did you spend your summer vacations? What did you like to do? Did you work during summer breaks or hang around with your friends?

49. Did you ever go away to camp? How old were you? What sort of a camp? Where was it located? What experiences did you have? Did you get homesick?

50. During the school year did you hold down a job? Were you expected to work?

51. Where did you work? What were your duties? How much were you paid per hour? What did you do with the money you earned?

52. What clothes and hairstyles were popular when you were a teen? Did you ever bleach or dye your hair or get a weird haircut? What was it like?

53. Did you ever volunteer while in high school? What did you do?

54. Did you consider yourself outgoing or shy? Did your friends consider you the life of the party?

55. Did you get along with the boys or the girls better? What sorts of kids made up your group of friends?

56. Did you keep a diary or a journal? Did you write in it regularly? Did anyone ever read your diary without permission? How did you respond?

57. Did you have a favorite high school hangout? Where was it and what did you do there?

58. How old were you before you began dating? Do you think you were too young or were you ready to date? What was your curfew?

59. How did your parents feel about you dating? What did they like or dislike about your dating choices? Did they ever disapprove of or forbid you to see someone? Why?

60. Where did you go on your first date and with whom?

61. Did you ever go steady? How old were you the first time? What was his or her name? Did you exchange class rings? Did you wear his or her ring on your finger or on a chain around your neck?

62. Did most of your friends go steady? Did you feel left out when you were not going steady or dating?

63. Where did you and your friends like to go on dates? Did you like to go in a group or double date? Did your date own a car or was a parent's car used?

64. How old were you when you learned to drive? Who taught you? Did you learn in a car or a pickup truck? Was it a stick shift or an automatic?

65. At what age did you get your first driver's license? In what city and state did you take and pass the test?

66. Did you study for the test? Did you have to take it more than once? Whose car did you use to take your driver's test?

67. Did you have your own car in high school? What year and model was it? Did you pay for the car yourself or was it a gift? Did you pay for your own insurance? Did you take care of it yourself?

68. What were your favorite songs, bands, and entertainers while in high school? Did you and your friends go to concerts or big band dances?

69. What month and year did you graduate from high school? Did you receive any special honors or scholarships? Were you a speaker?

70. How did you celebrate after graduation? What friends and relatives attended? Did you receive a special gift?

71. What did you do after high school graduation? Go to work? Marry? Go away to school? Take time off?

72. How would you describe your personality while in high school?

73. What incidents from your school days are still vivid in your memory?

74. What is the one thing you most regret doing as a teenager? Have you gotten over it?

75. What is your most memorable high school moment?

76. Do you believe that those were the best years of your life?

19

*God gave us memories
so that we might have roses in December.*

~ Barrie ~

College Years

1. When and where did you attend college? In what year did you graduate? What was your major? What degree did you earn? Did you ever change your major?

2. Did you win any accolades? Were you a valedictorian, magna or summa cum laude? What certificates did you earn?

3. Who attended your graduation? How did you celebrate?

4. Did anyone famous or infamous attend college with you or graduate from the same college?

5. Did you work your way through college? What type of work did you do? Do you remember how much you earned per hour?

6. Did you receive any financial assistance, loans or scholarships? Do you remember how much tuition was each semester?

7. Was it important to your family that you attend college? How important was getting a college education to you? Who else in your family graduated from college or were you the first?

8. Did you live in a dorm, an apartment, or a boarding house? Describe your living quarters. Did you share your living space with anyone? If so, what was it like?

9. Was that the first time you had lived away from home? Did you get homesick or lonesome for your hometown and friends? Did you call home often? How often were you able to go home?

10. Did you enjoy the freedom being away from home allowed? Did you make special friends and stay in touch through the years?

11. Did you make friends from other cultures and countries? What did you learn from them? Are any still your friends today?

12. Did you join a fraternity or sorority? What took place during rush week? What was its symbol? Do you still have your sorority or fraternity pin or other souvenirs?

13. In what way, if any, did belonging to a sorority or fraternity help you once you graduated?

14. Did you get involved in campus politics? What was the political atmosphere? In what demonstrations and campaigns did you get involved?

15. In what ways did college change you? Did you like the change? Did your family and friends notice a change in you?

16. What activities did you and your friends get involved in on the weekends?

17. Did you attend and support college team events? Which was your favorite sport?

18. Did you play a team sport? What position and how many years did you play?

19. Were you ever a cheerleader or on the pep squad? What was the experience like for you?

20. Did you date often in college? Do you remember any special dates or names of those you dated? Did you meet your future mate there?

21. Did you party a lot or were you more the studious type?

22. What were the fads or styles while in college? Did you keep up with fads or did you have your own particular style? Describe what you liked to wear.

23. Was there a particular professor or other person that made a lasting impression on you or inspired you to achieve your goals?

24. What was your grade average when you graduated? Was it tough keeping your average up or did learning come easy for you? How many hours a day did you have to study in order to maintain your grades?

25. How do you feel today about your education? Have you used it to your advantage? Do you feel it was a wise investment of time and money? Would you want the same thing for your children?

26. Do you feel colleges today are doing a better or worse job of educating than they were when you attended? In what ways?

20

He that raises a large family does, indeed,
while he lives to observe them, stands a
broader mark for sorrow; but then he stands
a broader mark for pleasure too.
~ Benjamin Franklin ~

Married with (or without) Children

1. What is your current home address?

2. Are you married? Widowed? Divorced?

3. What is your spouse's full name, place and date of birth?

4. How many brothers and sisters does you spouse have? What are their names?

5. What are the names of your spouse's parents?

6. Where do they live? How often do you get together with them?

7. Are they involved in the lives of your children?

8. What is your wife's maiden name?

9. Was this the first marriage for both of you?

10. If you've been divorced or widowed, what other last names did you go by?

11. Where did each of you live before you were married?

12. What month, day and year were you married? How many years have you been married? How do you like to celebrate your anniversary?

13. In what city and state were you were married? Was it a church, courthouse, or other? Who officiated at the ceremony?

14. How old were you and you spouse when you married? Do you feel you were too young to marry?

15. Did you have a large formal wedding or was it private? Who gave the bride away? What did you wear?

16. What are the names of your attendants? Who was your flower girl and ring bearer? What styles and colors did the attendants wear? Do you still keep in contact with anyone who was in the bridal party?

17. What kinds of flowers did you have? What music was played?

18. Who helped you plan your wedding? Did you or a parent pay for your wedding? What was the cost?

19. Do you have a wedding album? Do you ever look through it?

20. Where was the reception held? Describe your wedding cake. Did you toast with champagne? Who caught the bouquet?

21. How many guests attended your wedding? Who were the out-of-town or special guests that attended?

22. What sorts of wedding gifts did you receive? Did you return or exchange any of them?

23. Did you have a honeymoon? Where did you go and where did you stay? Have you ever revisited your honeymoon location?

24. If you eloped, what were the reasons? What were your parents' reactions to your elopement? Was it something you planned or was it a spur of the moment decision?

25. After the honeymoon where did you live? What type of furniture did you own?

26. What are the most memorable moments of your first five years of marriage?

27. Did you ever live with your parents as a married couple, if so, for how long?

28. What does your present home look like? What style is it?

29. What are the rooms of your home like? How do you have them decorated? What type of furniture do you have? Which is your favorite room?

30. What is your yard like? Do you have a swimming pool or children's play yard?

31. Do you entertain often? What sort of entertaining do you like to do? Do you like to have sit-down dinners or serve buffet style?

32. How do you celebrate Thanksgiving and religious holidays?

33. Do you decorate your home during the holidays? Do you decorate the outside of your home with lights?

34. Did your children participate in the decorating? What was their favorite part? Was there a ritual of sorts that they liked to follow?

35. At whose home are holiday meals usually held? When they are held at your home, do you do all the cooking or does everyone pitch in?

36. When you were first married what was your biggest concern?

37. Did you work when you were first married? What did you do? How long did you work before having children?

38. How many children do you have? What are their names and dates of birth?

39. How old were you when each child was born? How long were you married before you had your first child?

40. Do you remember the names of the obstetrician and pediatrician?

41. Did you work outside the home while raising your children? What did you do? Who took care of your children? What was the cost of childcare?

42. Did you read or sing to your children? Did they have a favorite story or song?

43. What about parenting brought you the most joy?

44. What do you consider to be your biggest mistake as a parent?

45. Were you active in the PTA? How did you participate? Did you attend open houses at your children's school?

46. Did you make sure that their homework was done each night and their grades kept up? Did you help them with their homework?

47. Were you a room mother or a teacher's aide? Did you ever coach their team sports?

48. Were your children in Boy Scouts or Girls Scouts or other organizations? What badges did they earn? Did you take part and get involved?

49. If your children were home schooled why did you choose to home school? What experiences did you have? How did they benefit? Did the children adjust and enjoy home schooling?

50. Do you own your home? What year did you purchase it? What was the purchase price? What was the interest rate at the time of purchase? What were your house payments each month? Did you both have to work to meet expenses?

51. Have you ever built and designed your own home from scratch? Was it a satisfying experience?

52. Do you feel safe in your neighborhood? Do you belong to a neighborhood watch? Do you lock your doors each time you leave the house and while at home?

53. Does your community or city experience much crime? What do you believe to be the biggest problem?

54. Do you attend church regularly? What denomination? Do you take part in the services?

55. What is the name and location of your church? What is your pastor's or rabbi's name?

56. Have you ever changed religions? What was the reason?

57. Do you study the Bible? What is your favorite passage? Is there a particular time of day that you like reading the Bible?

58. What did you and your spouse like to do together before you had children? Did you go dancing or to the movies? What kind of dancing did you do? What kind of movies did you enjoy? What was the cost of admission?

59. What events were taking place in the world when you were first married?

21

Nobody can do for little children
what grandparents do.
Grandparents sort of sprinkle stardust
over the lives of little children.

~ Alex Haley ~

Grandparents

1. What are the full names of your mother's and father's parents?

2. What are their dates and places of birth?

3. When and where were they married?

4. In what city and state (or country) were they born? If another county, from where and when did they come to America?

5. How did they arrive in the U.S.? At what airport or port did they land?

6. What do you know about their life in another country?

7. How did they dress? Did they follow any Old World customs?

8. Did they learn the English language? Did you learn to speak theirs?

9. Did you have a special name that you called your grandparents?

10. Where did they live? Did a grandparent ever live with you in your home?

11. How much were your grandparents involved in your life as a child?

12. What do you remember most about them?

13. What did your grandfather do for a living? Did your grandmother work outside the home? What did she do?

14. Did a grandparent serve in the military? What branch? What was his or her rank and how many years did they serve? Were they ever wounded while serving?

15. Did your grandparents graduate from high school and college?

16. How did the Great Depression and world wars affect them? Did they about talk it? Did they have stories from the prohibition era?

17. Did they have a favorite saying or cliche that you heard often?

18. Did they have any idiosyncrasies or strong beliefs?

19. Did your grandparents own their own home? Did they like to work in the garden? Did they like to travel or stay close to home?

20. Did you visit them often? What did you like to do while you visited? Did you like to spend the night?

21. What did your grandmother cook or bake that you especially liked? Did you ever help her?

22. What special thing did you learn from them that you never forgot?

23. If your grandparents are no longer living, how old were they when they passed away? What year? What was the cause of death?

24. How did you feel about their passing? How did you cope with their death? How old were you at the time?

25. Did a grandparent live in a convalescent home? How did you feel about them being there? Did you visit them often?

26. What are your thoughts on the possibility of having to live in a convalescent home someday?

27. Do you have grandchildren and great grandchildren? What are their names and ages?

22

*The bond that links your true family
is not one of blood, but of respect
and joy in each other's life . . .*
~ Richard Bach, Author ~

Military Life

1. In what branch of the military did you serve? What was your job?

2. Were you drafted into service or did you enlist? Where and on what date were you sworn into service?

3. What was your rank and serial number?

4. Where did you go for basic training? What was the name and location of the base? How far away from your hometown was it?

5. Did you find boot camp difficult or was it more or less what you expected? What vivid memory do you have from your boot camp days?

6. Were you ever ordered to do something difficult (like digging a six-foot hole) for discipline? What was the reason for the discipline?

7. Did you like wearing your uniform? What did it look like? Do you still have it?

8. How did you find barrack life? Did it take long to adjust to rising early?

9. Did you like military food? What foods did you miss most from home?

10. What was the name of your company? What duties were you assigned?

11. Did you have KP duty or drive in the motor pool?

12. Who was president and vice-president of the United States during your time of service?

13. Was there a war or conflict taking place? If so, in what years did they take place?

14. Were you shipped out to another country or were you stateside? What country or where in the U.S. were you stationed? What do you remember the most about the location?

15. Did you get homesick? Did you have someone back home to write to? What sorts of packages from home did you receive?

16. Did you ever get a Dear John letter? Who was it from and what were the reasons?

17. Were you ever in combat? Did you suffer any injuries? What were the injuries? How did they occur?

18. Did you spend time in a veteran's hospital or another hospital? Where was it located? How long were you there? Where did you go when you were released?

19. Did you find actual combat much different from what you were told or what you thought it would be like?

20. What was your most frightening moment? Did you ever feel you would die? Did you ever see a buddy die? How did you handle these moments?

21. Do you think training maneuvers prepared you physically and emotionally for what you experienced?

22. Did you or someone else in your company exhibit an extraordinary act of bravery? What was it?

23. What medals or citations did you receive?

24. Where did you and your buddies like to go for R&R? Did you spend it with wild abandon or good wholesome fun? Did anyone get into trouble?

25. Were you ever entertained by USO troops? Who were the entertainers? Did it help morale?

26. Did you hang photos of loved ones and pin-up girls in your barracks?

27. What date were you discharged? Where did you go after leaving the base?

28. Who was there to greet you? What sort of welcome home did you receive?

29. What did you do on your first night and day at home? Did you go to see old friends or stick around with family?

30. What was most difficult about adjusting to civilian life?

31. Did you have a job to come home to? Did you return to school?

32. What do you think about when you look back on those years?

33. Do you ever discuss that period of your life with your children or grandchildren?

34. What are your thoughts on war and serving your country?

35. Do you stay in contact with any of your buddies? Do you ever get together?

36. Are you an active member of a veteran's organization?

37. Did you ever consider making a career of the service? If you did make it your career how many years did you serve?

23

The history of the world is not complete
until your history is written.

~Unknown~

More About You

1. What words would you use to describe yourself? How would you describe your personality today? Do you think that others see you the way you see yourself?

2. How many jobs have you held in your lifetime? Which did you like the best?

3. Have you ever been without work or a place to live? Have you ever been completely broke? What were the circumstances? What did you do?

4. Have you ever broken any bones? Which ones? How did it happen? How old were you?

5. What operations have you had? What were the circumstances? How old were you?

6. Have you ever been hospitalized for something other than surgery? For what reason? How old were you?

7. Do you get anxious when you visit a doctor or dentist's office? Did you ever have a medical experience that frightened you?

8. What is the name of your doctor, dentist, and ophthalmologist? Do you visit a chiropractor? Do you practice a holistic approach to health?

9. Are you allergic to any insects, pollens, animals, foods or medications?

10. Have you ever smoked cigarettes, cigars, or a pipe? What brand? Do you remember any cigarette company slogans?

11. At what age did you begin smoking? If you quit, how old were you? How much did you pay for a pack of cigarettes at that time?

12. Was smoking the "in-thing" to do when you were young?

13. What foreign language do you speak? Do you speak it at home or on the job?

14. Are you right or left handed, or are you ambidextrous?

15. Have you ever had an automobile accident? What were the circumstances?

16. Who was the U.S. President the first time you voted? How old were you? Did you understand the issues? Where did you vote? What was the voting booth and voting procedure like at that time?

17. With what party are you affiliated? Do you tend to vote as your parents voted?

18. Have you ever switched parties? What were the reasons?

19. Do you vote in each election? Where do you go to vote? Do you use the absentee ballot? Have you ever worked a precinct?

20. What campaign slogans have you remembered over the years?

21. Do you get involved in local politics? Have you ever run for political office? What office did you run for? Did you have a tough opponent? Did you win or lose?

22. Did you like campaigning and talking about the issues? Who helped you with your campaign? What were some of your experiences as a candidate? Would you run again?

23. What newspapers do you like to read? What radio stations do you listen to? What television stations do you watch? Do you read or listen to the news everyday?

24. What section of the newspaper is your favorite? Do you like to work the crossword puzzle and read the comics?

25. Do you own a computer? What kind and brand? What do you use it for the most? What other electronic and technical equipment do you own?

26. Have you ever lived in another country? For what reasons were you there? How did you adjust to the culture and the people? What did you like the most? Did you learn to speak the language?

27. Have you ever backpacked or biked across the United States or another country? How far did you travel? Were there any mishaps along the way? What did you learn?

28. Do you like to spend time alone or do you like having others around? What sorts of things do you like to do when you're alone?

29. Do you have close friends that you meet with often? What do you like to talk about or do when you're together?

30. What types of books do you enjoy reading? Who is your favorite author? How many books do you read in one year?

31. What talents do you possess? How much do they mean to you? How much time do you spend on them?

32. What do you consider to be your biggest achievement at this point in your life?

33. Is there something special that you want to accomplish? Do you believe you will? Are you currently working on making it happen?

34. As an adult, have you ever wanted to go back to school? Did you? What did you study and why?

35. Do you practice Karate or another martial art? How serious are you about the art? Are you competitive?

24

*There have been great societies that did not
use the wheel but there have been
no societies that did not tell stories.*

~ Unknown ~

Odds and Ends

1. If you had the opportunity would you go into space?

2. Do you own and display the American flag?

3. Do you have a motto or creed that you live by?

4. What is your favorite quotation? Do you like to collect quotes?

5. Have you ever written a letter to the editor of a newspaper? What was it about?

6. Do you drive the same route every day to work? What streets do you take?

7. What grocery stores do you like to frequent? What is your grocery budget? Is it easy to stick to or do you often go over budget?

8. What department stores do you frequent? Do you have charge accounts or do you always pay cash? Do you like to shop?

9. How much do you spend on your wardrobe each season? Do you donate unwanted items? Do you have a favorite charity?

10. What style of clothes do you like to wear? Classic or casual? What style of shoes do you like? What color looks best on you?

11. Do or did you ever wear hats and gloves?

12. Do you dress up when you dine out or attend church? Do you ever wear evening gowns or a tux?

13. Do you wear suits and ties to work?

14. What is the name and location of the barbershop or hair salon that you patronize? How long have you been going there?

15. What do you pay for haircuts and permanents?

16. Do you have a full head of hair or are you bald? Does balding run in the family?

17. What is the best advice you ever received? Who was it from? Did you follow it?

18. What are you like when you're sick? Do you like to have someone care for you or do you like to be left alone?

19. Do you believe in the "good ol' days"?

20. Do you own a gun? What kind? Do you hunt or target shoot?

21. Do you think that children understand the history of their country? Did you understand it when you were young?

22. Do you believe that today's children are smarter than their parents were at their age?

23. Have you ever attended the Olympics? Which one and where was it held?

24. Have you taken part in the Olympics or wanted to be an Olympic athlete? In what sport?

25. Have you ever attended a World's Fair? Where and when?

26. Of all the cars or trucks you've owned which one was your favorite? What year, model, and color was it? How long did you own it?

27. What do you keep in the glove compartment and in the trunk of you vehicle? Are you usually prepared for emergencies?

28. Do you like to get into your car or truck and just drive without a particular destination?

29. Do you send your laundry out or do it yourself? What brand of laundry soap do you use? What is the name of the laundromat and dry cleaners you patronize?

30. Are you a list keeper? What sorts of lists do you make? Do you stick to them?

31. Do you keep a calendar for all your appointments, birthdays and anniversaries?

32. Have you ever experienced an earthquake, tornado, or other type of disaster? What was it like?

33. What do you think about the space program? Where were you at the time of the Challenger and Columbia tragedies? How did you react to these tragedies?

34. Are you mechanically inclined? What sort of mechanics?

35. What superstitions do you have?

36. Do you believe in astrology or numerology? Do you read your daily horoscope?

37. Have you ever visited a psychic or a numerologist?

38. Do you play the lottery? What is the most money you've won?

39. Do you like to gamble? Would you consider yourself a risk-taker?

40. Do you make New Year's resolutions and stick to them?

41. What is your favorite recipe? Share it with your family here or on another sheet of paper.

42. Do you consider yourself a gourmet cook? Who taught you how to cook or did you learn on your own?

43. What do you usually eat for breakfast? Is it eaten on the run or do you sit at the table?

44. Do you drink coffee or tea?

45. Do you like to go out for breakfast or brunch on weekends? Do you eat out often? What is your favorite restaurant?

46. Do you know your neighbors by name? Do you visit?

47. When a new neighbor moves in, do you welcome them into the neighborhood?

48. Do you have a vegetable or flower garden? Do you spend a lot of time there? Do you hire a gardener or do everything yourself? Do you attend garden shows?

49. What time of night do you usually go to bed?

50. Do you like to read, watch TV, or take a hot bath before going to bed?

51. What brand of toothpaste and soap do you use?

52. Do you keep your photographs in albums or are they stuffed in drawers or boxes? Do you like to look through them from time to time?

53. What kinds of pets do you have? Have you always had pets? Do you travel with them?

54. What is the most exotic pet you've owned?

55. Where is your favorite vacation spot? Do you go there regularly?

56. Do you have a daily or weekly routine? What is it?

57. Do you have a savings account? Do you consider yourself frugal?

58. Do you have a container where you keep loose change?

59. What year was your favorite? What was your favorite age to be?

60. Have you ever worn braces? How old were you?

61. Are you interested in history? What years interest you the most?

62. How would you like to be remembered?

25

Life is hurrying past us and running away,
too strong to stop, too sweet to lose.
~ Willa Cather, Author ~

What do you Remember?

1. Charles Lindbergh's flight to Paris

2. The bombing of Pearl Harbor, Internment camps

3. War Bonds, the stock market, food lines

4. Prohibition, speakeasies, and flappers

5. Assassination of President John Kennedy, Robert Kennedy, Dr. Martin Luther King

6. Flagpole sitting, goldfish swallowing, phone booth stuffing

7. The Beatles coming to America, streakers

8. Coffee shops with tableside jukeboxes

9. Home milk delivery, glass milk bottles with cardboard stoppers

10. Ice delivery for ice boxes, metal ice trays with levers

11. Oleo margarine made from lard and orange coloring

12. S & H Green Stamps, Blue Chip Stamps

13. Ration stamps during WWII

14. The Civil Rights Movement, The Cuban missile crisis

15. Drive-in restaurants and carhops

16. Metal clamp-on skates, roller skate keys

17. Rainbow popsicles and lemonade stands

18. Electric-powered streetcars on tracks

19. Black and white television and hi-fi

20. Helm's Bakery delivery trucks in neighborhoods

21. Wax Coke-shaped bottles with sugar water inside

22. Soda machines that dispensed glass bottles

23. Uniformed theatre ushers with flashlights

24. Drive-in movie theatres, Disneyland opens in California

25. Newsreels and live music before a movie

26. 45 and $33^1/3$ RPM records, 8-track tapes

27. Music store listening booths, rock and roll

28. Passenger trains with dining cars and sleeping berths

29. Blackjack, clove chewing gum and candy cigarettes

30. Rubik's cube, Quija boards and Slinky

31. Driving hand signals before indicators

32. Headlight dimmer switches on floorboard and curb feelers

33. Gasoline at 35¢ per gallon, bread at four loaves for $1.00

34. Minimum wage 50¢ per hour

35. First class postage 3¢, postcards 1¢, twice-a-day mail delivery.

36. Bonus gifts in boxes of laundry soap, floral flour sacks

37. The first TV dinners and TV trays

38. Stores closing nights and weekends

39. Poodle skirts, crinoline slips, saddle shoes and stiletto heels

40. Ducktail haircuts, bouffant hairstyles, butch wax

41. McCarthy hearings and the Hollywood blacklist

42. Burma-Shave wooden roadside signs

43. High school car clubs, sock hops, and proms

44. Flowered swimming caps and one-piece bathing suits

45. Peashooters, BB guns, and homemade sling shots

46. Howdy Doody, Captain Kangaroo, Cecil the Seasick Sea Serpent, Crusader Rabbit

47. Mimeograph, carbon paper, typewriters and ink wells

48. Rotary telephones, phone numbers with word pre-fixes and party lines

49. "Kilroy was here" painted on rocks and walls

50. Fallout shelters, air raids and drills

51. Water cooler bags on cars

52. Saturday morning radio adventure shows and radio soap operas

53. WPA (Works Progress Administration, 1936)

54. Sky King, Inner Sanctum, The Shadow, Charlie Chan, Terry and the Pirates

55. Sputnik, sending monkeys into space

56. Lost in Space TV series, black and white cartoons

57. Wagon Train and Death Valley Days TV shows

58. Fred Allen, Burns and Allen, Jack Benny, Great Gildersleeve, Minnie Pearl

59. Buster Brown and his Dog Tige, The Phillip Morris boy

60. Arthur Godfrey's Talent Scouts and The Original Amateur Hour

61. Box shutter cameras and blue flashbulbs

62. Outhouses, kerosene lamps, coal delivery, coal bins

63. Polio epidemic, sugar cube oral vaccine, discovery of Penicillin

64. Studebakers, Edsels, Hudsons, Packards, DeSotos

65. Washboards and wringer washing machines

66. Clotheslines and wood cooking stoves

67. Hula hoops and paper dolls

68. John L. Sullivan, Jackie Robinson, Knute Rockne

69. F. W. Woolworth lunch counters

70. Ice cream parlors, drive-in restaurants with speakers

71. Irons and curling irons heated on the stove

72. Big bands: Benny Goodman, Tommy Dorsey, Glenn Miller

73. Jitterbug, The Twist, dance marathons

74. Original Tinker Toys and Lincoln Logs, slot cars, troll dolls

75. War songs: Till We meet Again, Over There, Don't Sit Under the Apple Tree

76. Victory gardens, tire and gas rationing

77. One-room schoolhouses and outhouses

78. Men's Nehru jackets and Zoot suits

79. Astronaut, Alan Shepard, first U.S. Space flight

80. Women's peasant skirts and go-go boots

81. Woodstock Festival, Haight Ashbury, East Village

82. Dr. Benjamin Spock's baby book, cloth diapers, and diaper pins

83. Kewpie and Cabbage Patch dolls, Chatty Cathy and G. I. Joe

84. Watergate, Berlin Wall, Bermuda Triangle

85. Peace signs, flower children, and earth shoes

86. Mustard plasters, castor oil remedies

87. 3-D Movies, reel to reel recorders

88. The Generation Gap and communes

89. Transistor radios, taps on shoes

90. Ziefield Follies, Fanny Brice, Vaudeville

91. Bowling alley pin (set up) boys

92. Smokey the Bear, New York City blackout, 1977

93. The Hindenberg disaster, 1936

94. Orson Welles's War of the Worlds radio drama

95. San Francisco earthquake 1989

96. Scopes Monkey Trial 1920s

97. Apollo moon landing, Woodstock Rock Festival

98. Sears & Roebuck and Montgomery Wards catalogs

99. Fuller Brush man, 100th birthday of Statue of Liberty, 1987

100. First test tube baby born 1978, total eclipse of the sun, 1979

26

Memories of our lives, of our words and our deeds will continue in others.

~ Rosa Parks ~

The List of Lists

This section is fun and it will get you thinking—maybe even rethinking—your thoughts and views. To make your list interesting and personal, give reasons for your responses.

This list is also a great conversation starter. The next time you find yourself seated along side a non-talker, think of a question from this list and jump start a conversation. Try this with your family too. It's a good way to learn how and what they think. You might be surprised.

1. List tangible possessions that you could not live without.

2. List places you'd like to visit if money were no object.

3. List famous people you'd like to invite to dinner.

4. List things you'd do if you were the President of the United States today.

5. List the values that you adhere to.

6. List the types of magazines you currently subscribe to.

7. List the projects you've started but never finished.

8. List the good ideas you've had that never happened.

9. List the good ideas you had that turned out well.

10. List what you'd do if you were the opposite sex.

11. List the most important lessons you have learned.

12. List things you wish you had never sold.

13. List things you would like your children to be or do with their lives.

14. List places you would go if you wanted to get away from it all.

15. List things you would do if money were no object.

16. List things that you would like to change about yourself.

17. List things you like best about yourself.

18. List souvenirs you have collected and always kept.

19. List what you believe the world could live without.

20. List the things you believe you could live without.

21. List things you like and do not like about modern technology.

22. List things that you would never say to anyone.

23. List the best things about being a grandparent.

24. List the things you most admire about your children.

25. List the things you would not change in your life.

26. List things you would hide if someone famous were coming to dinner.

27. List all the bridges you have burned over the years.

28. List the books that made a difference in your thinking or your life.

29. List risks you would take if you had absolutely no fear at all.

30. List things you did not do because of fear but wish you had.

31. List your proudest moments and accomplishments.

32. List any brushes with fame you've had.

33. List the famous or infamous people you have met or seen.

34. List any brushes with death you've had.

35. List the most important people in your life right now.

36. List things you feel people don't know about you.

37. List careers you would like to experiment with if you had the chance.

38. List what you like most about your spouse.

39. List the thing you want most for your grandchildren.

40. List the habits of others that annoy you the most.

41. List personal habits you would like to change.

42. List the things you like most about your home.

43. List things that make you feel uncomfortable.

44. List the things that make you the angriest.

45. List books you would like to read if you had time.

46. List people you would not consider entertaining in your home.

47. List the reasons you believe or do not believe in war.

48. List the fears you have for your family living in today's world.

49. List what you would change about the entertainment industry.

50. List reasons you would like to write a book.

51. List the things that make you restless and bored.

52. List compliments you've received and recall from time to time.

53. List the things you would do if you won the lottery.

54. List the reasons you think listening to others is important.

55. List the reasons you would or would not run for public office.

56. List things you would do first if you were to lose your job today.

57. List the things that make you smile and laugh out loud.

58. List people you thought you would marry but didn't.

59. List things in life that energize you.

60. List what you would do if you had only one year to live.

61. List ways that others make you feel appreciated.

62. List the ways you like to relax or meditate.

63. List things you wish you had been told as a child.

64. List the ways you notice your body changing as you age.

65. List your thoughts on aging.

66. List contests you've entered and won.

67. List the things you want to accomplish in your lifetime.

68. List the things that might prevent you from accomplishing your goals.

69. List places you think you would like to live when you retire.

70. List exotic or unusual places you dream about visiting.

71. List steps you would take to bring about world peace if you had the power.

72. List ways under which you learn the best.

73. List the worst parties you have given or attended.

74. List the reasons you would want to go into space.

75. List the most memorable gift you've ever received.

76. List the people you want to thank but have put off thanking.

77. List companies with which you would never do business.

78. List ways you believe crime and punishment should be approached.

79. List the most influential people in your life.

80. List reasons you feel people are apathetic.

81. List the men and women you most admire.

82. List excuses you have made to get out of situations.

83. List the things in life that amaze you the most.

84. List jobs you have liked and disliked the most.

85. List the most disappointing moments in your life.

86. List the number of times and ways you have dieted.

87. List how you would solve poverty and homelessness if you could.

88. List the things that make you feel guilty.

89. List the things you do extremely well.

90. List well-known families that you admire.

91. List other first names you would have chosen for yourself.

92. List the types of art you would like to create.

93. List your reasons why being famous can be good or bad.

94. List things you appreciate and like most about the animal world.

95. List what you believe you are on this Earth to do.

96. List the things you like to daydream about.

97. List what your spiritual beliefs mean to you.

98. List things you would tell your grandchildren if you had one last message to write them.

99. List reasons you believe that knowing one's heritage is important.

100. List why you want to write your life's stories.

"Write about what you know best . . . the days of your life."

Book List

Bird by Bird: Some Instructions on Writing and Life
    Anne Lamott
Cameo Life Stories: Writing Guide for Every Woman
    Deborah Hansen Linzer
Gifts from the Sea
    Anne Morrow Lindbergh
On Writing: A Memoir on the Craft of Writing
    Stephen King
Reaching Back
    Alice Chapin
Is There a Book Inside of You
    Dan Poynter
Writing Nonfiction: Turning Thoughts into Books
    Dan Poynter
The Story of Your Life: Writing a Spiritual Autobiography
    Dan Wakefield
Write Your Heart Out
    Rebecca McClanahan
Write Where You Live
    Elaine Fantle Shimberg
Writing Family Histories and Memoirs
    Kirk Polking
Inventing the Truth: The Art and Craft of Memoir
    William Zinsser
The Photo Scribe
    Denis Ledoux

Turning Memories into Memoirs
Denis Ledoux

Exploring Our Lives
Francis E. Kazemek

Portrait of Myself
Margaret Bourke-White

An American Childhood
Annie Dillard

The Times of My Life
Betty Ford

The Diary of a Young Girl
Anne Frank

Story of My Life
Helen Keller

On My Own
Eleanor Roosevelt

One Writer's Beginnings
Eudora Welty

Creating Poetry
John Drury

Guidelines for Preserving Your Photographic Heritage
Ralph G. McKnight

Preserving Your Family Photographs
Maureen A. Taylor

How to Publish and Market Your Family History
Carl Boyer III

Your Life in Print Story by Story
Pat Cuellar

Internet Resources

As of this printing the following resources are active, however, Internet changes are frequent. If you're unable to connect to an address listed, type in the title you need on your search engine and a new address should appear.

Writers Resource Center, www.poewar.com

Yahoo Dictionaries, www.yahoo.com/reference/dictionaries

Library of Congress Copyright Office, www.loc.gov

Elements of Style, www.bartleby.com/strunk/141

— Writing Magazines —

Family Tree Magazine, www.familytreemagazine.com

Family Chronicle, www.familychronicle.com

Writer's Digest, www.writersdigest.com

Writing Etc., www.FilbertPublishing.com

Reminisce Magazine, www.reminisce.com

— Online Bookstores —

Amazon.com, www.amazon.com

Barnes & Noble.com, www.barnesandnoble.com

— Genealogy —

Cyndi's List, www.cyndislist.com

FamilySearch (LDS), www.familysearch.org

RootsWeb.com, www.rootsweb.com

Ancestry.com, www.ancestry.com

Internet Resources

— Time Lines (great fun to read through) —

American Cultural History: The Twentieth Century,
http://kclibrary.nhmccd.edu/decades.html

PBS History (time lines and virtual tours),
www.pbs.org/neighborhoods/history/

Timelines of History,
www.timelines.ws/20thcent/TWENTIETHCENT

— Print-on-Demand Publishers —

1stBooks, www.1stbooks.com

Xlibris, www.xlibris.com

IUniverse, www.iuniverse.com

Trafford Publishing, www.trafford.com

— Archival & Services —

The Preservation Station, www.preservesmart.com

Light Impressions, www.lightimpressiondirect.com

D'Marie, www.dmarie.com

— Organizations —

International Women's Writing Guild, www.iwwg.com

The National Association of Women Writers, www.naww.org

Association of Personal Historians, www.personalhistorians.org

Small Publishers, Artists & Writers, www.SPAWN.org

Order: Your Life in Print

Place your book order at: www.LifePrintsPublishing.com
Or send check or money order to:

Pat Cuellar
LifePrints Publishing
432 La Costa Circle
Dayton, NV 89403

$12.95 per book

Add 7.25% for books shipped to California addresses

Shipping by air: US: $3.50 for first book
                                   $2.00 for each additional book
International: (estimate) $9.00 for first book
                                   $5.00 for each additional book

Please PRINT all information

Your name:_____

Address: _____

City: _____

State: _____ Zip: _____

Telephone: (_____)_____

Fax: _____

E-mail: _____

☐ **Check here for book signed by the author**
☐ **Check here for gift card with your name**

Recipient's name: _____

Print additional orders on a separate sheet

Thank You for Your Order!